Pieces of storm

Storm Royal

Presentation by *BookLeaf Publishing*

Web: www.bookleafpub.com

E-mail: info@bookleafpub.com

ISBN: 9789395756549

First edition 2022

DEDICATION

To christabelle

Who relentlessly made an effort to find me,when I couldn't find myself.

ACKNOWLEDGEMENT

I would like to acknowledge, and give my warmest thanks to bookleaf publishing who has made this possible.

I would like to show gratitude to my best friend,who has been insanely supportive. And also give special thanks to asher,who has relentlessly encouraged me to pursue this all the way.

Finally,I would like to thank God for sustaining me and making believe this was possible.

PREFACE

I have decided to take a chance and write this book,drawing from the up and down experiences I've had in life.

This is a book of poems,that realistically tells stories that most people do experience. Love,pain,encouragement and growth. I hope in one way or the other,it resonates with you as you read.

My pen

I picked up my pen,
And inked the pages of my journal,
With my emotions.
And it was liberating .

For once,
I was heard.
For once,
I may be understood.

Halves of a whole

I am part,
And you are part.
I say you are day to my night,
You say I am peace to your troubles .
I say you are rain to my drought,
You say I am heaven to your earth.

I wonder,
How one so phenomenal can exist.
I've loved,
I love,
And I'll always love you.
Till the heavens are stunned,
And the earth is rid of it's skies.

Halves of a whole.

Closure

I was so damn sure,
I'd keep these memories forever .
But alas,
Like drops of rain,
Tricking down my window from a light drizzle,
You slowly fade.
I can't remember your first confession,
I'm not sure which was our last kiss.
And even scarier,
I'm not anxious to remember .
This must be what it feels like,
To finally find closure.

Daggers

His words flew like daggers,
Piercing my heart,
Carving away my fortitude,
Layer by layer,
Till nothing but the sob I held back in my throat,
Could be felt.
And it hurt,
In a way I couldn't explain.

Filth

Undo what you did.
Wipe my heart clean,
Of this filth called pain,
That sickens my happiness .

Winter

6

How do I covet you?
I can't .
How do I mourn you?
I also can't .
You were the winter breeze,
In the summer of my life,
Refreshing...yet fleeting.

Fell

This is enough for me.
To know that on this day,
In this very moment ,
I fell...
For you,
As nature witnessed.

Spill

Once ,
Just this Once,
I'll shed this tears.
Knowing each drop of emotion,
That spills from my eyes ,
Is my heart willful attempt,
To rid itself,
Of all it felt for you.

Mad phenomenon

I'd like to think ,
Our love defied every rule and theory.
It was wild,
It was calm.
It was beautiful,
And it was ugly.
It was every part of you and me,
A beautiful mess,
A mad phenomenon.

Dazzle

I tried to forget,
Every sad memory of us,
But I couldn't.
When we cried,
When we fought.
When we cuddled,
When we laughed.
Even when we stared from a distance.
Every moment we had dazzled,
Cause you were in it,
And I was happy.

You

Oh love,
Are you yet to understand?
I was lost to the world,
Drowning in anguish and darkness,
Gasping for air,
And scrambling for life,
Till I found you.

You were the world I so desperately craved.
The lifeline I clung to near death.
The light that illuminated my darkness.
And I've woven myself deep,
Into the vines of your heart.
To just say "I love you",
Would be a great injustice .

I love you,crave you,need you
"I am you"
So how can you even doubt how I feel?

I know

I know...
It's not just a feeling.

I see the sparkle in your eyes dwindle,
I hear your faint sighs,
When I initiate a conversation.

I see the way you avoid my touch.
You flee,
Like darkness from illumination.

I see your indifference,
When I shed tears,
And lay on the cold bed by myself.

I know...
You don't love me anymore.

World

I penned it down,
The first time my heart skipped for you.
Giddy-like and thrilling,
You intrigued me.

I wrote a poem,
When you told me you loved me.
My heart wouldn't stop racing,
Skipping away into the sunset.

I wrote a story,
When this world took you.
Ripping my heart to shreds,
And burying my happiness.
My heart would beat for you no longer.

I wove an entire world for you,
Through my words.
But you aren't even here to see it.

Hope

Oh dear one,
Take heed now,
Of the words you speak.
Do not birth hope,
Only to let it die.

You speak of a love unconditional,
Not a mere emotion.
Not just a physicality,
But a phenomenon
That transcends lifetimes.

You boldly promise.
Such heavy words,
But would you really?

Would you love me,
If I lost the beauty that entices you so?
Or became disfigured by a deformity?

Would you love me,
If this personality changed?
Or sickness crippled me to the core?

Would you love me beyond death?

When I become nothing,
But a figment of your imagination,
A memory.

Would you love me?
When everything is not as it was,
And the time of youth has waned?

Take heed dear one.
Do not birth hope,
Only to let it die.

Evidence

Scars...
The evidence that he was here.

My skin,
A landmark of his cruelty.
Oh the fool I was.

I giggled,
As he trailed my skin with kisses.
Each kiss,searing my skin,
With broken parts of him,
I didn't know existed.

Pain,anger,abuse.
Betrayal,obsession,manipulation.

I smiled,till I cried,and I prayed.
I prayed,till I smiled,and I laughed.

I'll wear this scars like badges of honour,
With pride, and confidence.

This is the evidence of my survival.

Torn

When we spilt,
A world was torn apart.

The sun hid and gave no light.
The skies darkened in sadness.
The moon dimmed,
And gave no comfort.
The stars retreated,
And the clouds wept endlessly for us.

Rose

Make no haste to disregard me,
Shriveled as I may seem,
This is not my end.

Like a rose,
I bloomed beautifully in spring.
Wilted in the summer,
And shriveled up in winter.

But spring...will come again.
And this rose,
Will bloom magnificently once more.

Loving you

Pretty little thing,
You must know,
Loving you is no simple journey .

There are good days ,
There are bad days.
The storm comes,
But the sun also shines.
When you're healing,
When you're broken.

It's an endless rollercoaster of emotions.
But I'm gonna be here,
For every ride.

Seeds

I'd like to believe,
These scars I wear so proudly,
Are seeds sown.

And one day,
When I'm strong enough,
These seeds will germinate.
They will grow,
And they will bloom,
Into the most beautiful flowers ever seen.
One day.

Child of lightening

And when you make it through the storm,
And emerge from what life thought would end
you,
Shine your light so bright.
For one kissed by lightening,
Cannot be shrouded by darkness.

Wild

And when all is said and done,
This spirit of mine will remain.

A little soft,
A little fragile.
A little wild,
A little bold.

And this lips of mine,
Will spin tales.
From now...till the end of time.

www.ingramcontent.com/pod-product-compliance
Lightning Source LLC
Chambersburg PA
CBHW060927130726
48001CB00006B/2463